D1134811

FAVOURITE VERSE

Edited by
STEVIE SMITH

CHANCELLOR
PRESS

First published in Great Britain by B.T. Batsford Limited
as *The Batsford Book of Children's Verse*

This edition published by Chancellor Press
59 Grosvenor Street
London W1

ISBN 0 907486 07 X

Selection © Stevie Smith 1970

Printed in Hong Kong

Preface

In selecting verses for this book I have followed my own tastes as they are now and as they were in my childhood. The first poem I ever learnt by heart was Shelley's 'Arethusa' and I thought it was a fine piece of work because of the extraordinary words in it and the dashing rhythm.

Childhood's thoughts can cut deep. I remember when I was about eight, for instance, thinking the road ahead might be rather too long, and being cheered by the thought, at that moment first occurring to me, that life lay in our hands. Many poems have been inspired by this thought, at least many of mine have.

Glancing finally through this anthology, I see I have picked a good deal from the late eighteenth and early nineteenth centuries . . . such 'romantics' as Shelley, Keats, Coleridge, Cowper, Byron, and of course Wordsworth. It was with pleasure I often picked out their fiercer poems. Keats' '*Why in the name of Glory were they proud?*' is a splendid line and a splendid taunt, against people who deserved taunting. So too with Shelley's Masque of Anarchy. I always liked the lines about Lord Eldon.

> *His big tears, for he wept well,*
> *Turned to mill-stones as they fell;*

> *And the little children, who*
> *Round his feet played to and fro,*
> *Thinking every tear a gem*
> *Had their brains knocked out by them.*

And of course Byron's beautifully *ratty* lines to Caroline Lamb. In kinder mood, and rather later on, there is Hardy's delightful picture of the defeated candidate's wife on her balcony. For me that little hand waves gamely forever.

On the whole, it is a pictured choice I have made, with the clouds, flowers, animals, trees, high seas and colours, to temper the shrillness of argument and give us peaceful feelings. Choosing these poems is a task I have enjoyed very much. I hope the reader will also enjoy himself.

STEVIE SMITH

3

Acknowledgment

The Author and Publishers would like to thank the following for
permission to include certain copyright poems:
ROBERT FROST, 'A Peck of Gold' and 'Acquainted with the Night'
(from *The Complete Poems of Robert Frost*): Messrs Holt,
Rinehart and Winston Inc, New York, and Messrs Jonathan
Cape Ltd, London
THOMAS HARDY, 'The Rejected Member's Wife', 'The Ruined
Maid' and 'Midnight on the Great Western' (from *The Col-
lected Poems of Thomas Hardy*): The Trustees of the Hardy
Estate, Messrs Macmillan and Co. Ltd, London, and The
Macmillan Company, New York
RUDYARD KIPLING, 'The Other Man' (from *Plain Tales from the
Hills*): Mrs George Bambridge, Macmillan and Co. Ltd,
London, and Doubleday and Co. Inc., New York
STEVIE SMITH, 'The Old Sweet Dove of Wiveton, Norfolk' (from
Selected Poems): Longman Group Ltd, London, and New
Directions, New York; 'The Frog Prince' (from *The Frog
Prince*): Longman Group Ltd, London and (from *The Best
Beast*) Alfred A. Knopf, New York; 'The Occasional Yarrow'
and 'Hymn to the Seal' (from *The Frog Prince*): Longman
Group Ltd, London
W. B. YEATS, 'Two Songs of a Fool' (from *Collected Poems* of W. B.
Yeats): Mr M. B. Yeats, Macmillan and Co. Ltd, London, and
The Macmillan Company, New York.

Contents

The Illustrations

The publishers wish to thank the following for their kind permission to reproduce the photographs in this book:

A-Z Botanical Collection, 21; Californian Institute of Technology, 33; Bruce Coleman/Reinhard, 53; J E Downward, 25; Tony Evans cover, 73; Explorer/Cros, 45; Valerie Finnis, 57, 69; Frank Lane (H. Schremp) 65; Natural History Photographic Agency/Tweedie, 77; Northern Ireland Tourist Board, 49; Spectrum Colour Library, 29; Mike St Maur Shiel, 41; Tony Stone Associates Ltd, 37; Trevor Wood, 61; Zefa, 17.

From– The Strayed Reveller

T HESE things, Ulysses,
The wise Bards also
Behold and sing.
But oh, what labour!
O Prince, what pain!

They too can see
Tiresias:—but the Gods,
Who gave them vision,
Added this law:
That they should bear too
His groping blindness,
His dark foreboding,
His scorn'd white hairs;
Bear Hera's anger
Through a life lengthen'd
To seven ages.

They see the Centaurs
On Pelion:—then they feel,
They too, the maddening wine
Swell their large veins to bursting; in wild pain
They feel the biting spears
Of the grim Lapithae, and Theseus, drive,
Drive crashing through their bones; they feel
High on a jutting rock in the red stream
Alcmena's dreadful son
Ply his bow:—such a price
The Gods exact for song;
To become what we sing.

MATTHEW ARNOLD

From– Psalm XIX

THE heavens declare the glory of God: and the firmament showeth his handvwork.

One day telleth another: and one night certifieth another.

There is neither speech nor language: but their voices are heard among them.

Their sound is gone out into all lands: and their words into the ends of the world.

In them hath he set a tabernacle for the sun: which cometh forth as a bridegroom out of his chamber, and rejoiceth as a giant to run his course.

It goeth forth from the uttermost part of the heaven, and runneth about unto the end of it again: and there is nothing hid from the heat thereof.

Ozymandias of Egypt

I MET a traveller from an antique land
Who said: Two vast and trunkless legs of stone
Stand in the desert. Near them, on the sand,
Half sunk, a shattered visage lies, whose frown
And wrinkled lip, and sneer of cold command
Tell that its sculptor well those passions read
Which yet survive, stamped on these lifeless things,
The hand that mocked them, and the heart that fed:
And on the pedestal these words appear:
'My name is Ozymandias, king of kings:
Look on my works, ye mighty, and despair!'
Nothing beside remains. Round the decay
Of that colossal wreck, boundless and bare,
The lone and level sands stretch far away.

PERCY BYSSHE SHELLEY

Catullan Hendecasyllables

Hear, my belovèd, an old Milesian story!—
High, and embosom'd in congregated laurels,
Glimmer'd a temple upon a breezy headland;
In the dim distance amid the skiey billows
Rose a fair island; the god of flocks had blest it.
From the far shores of the bleat-resounding island
Oft by the moonlight a little boat came floating,
Came to the sea-cave beneath the breezy headland,
Where amid myrtles a pathway stole in mazes
Up to the groves of the high embosom'd temple.
There in a thicket of dedicated roses,
Oft did a priestess, as lovely as a vision,
Pouring her soul to the son of Cytherea,
Pray him to hover around the slight canoe-boat,
And with invisible pilotage to guide it
Over the dusk wave, until the nightly sailor
Shivering with ecstasy sank upon her bosom.

SAMUEL TAYLOR COLERIDGE

Written in March
While resting on the bridge at the foot of Brother's Water

THE Cock is crowing,
The stream is flowing,
The small birds twitter,
The lake doth glitter,
The green field sleeps in the sun;
The oldest and youngest
Are at work with the strongest;
The cattle are grazing,
Their heads never raising;
There are forty feeding like one!

Like an army defeated
The snow hath retreated,
And now doth fare ill
On the top of the bare hill;
The ploughboy is whooping—anon—anon:
There's joy in the mountains;
There's life in the fountains;
Small clouds are sailing,
Blue sky prevailing;
The rain is over and gone!

WILLIAM WORDSWORTH

13

November

THE shepherds almost wonder where they dwell,
And the old dog for his right journey stares:
The path leads somewhere, but they cannot tell,
And neighbour meets with neighbour unawares.
The maiden passes close beside her cow,
And wanders on, and thinks her far away;
The ploughman goes unseen behind his plough
And seems to lose his horses half the day.
The lazy mist creeps on in journey slow;
The maidens shout and wonder where they go;
So dull and dark are the November days.
The lazy mist high up the evening curled,
And now the morn quite hides in smoke and haze;
The place we occupy seems all the world.

JOHN CLARE

From– The Masque of Anarchy

WHAT is Freedom?—ye can tell
That which Slavery is too well—
For its very name has grown
To an echo of your own.

'Tis to work and have such pay
As just keeps life from day to day
In your limbs, as in a cell
For your tyrants' use to dwell.

So that ye for them are made,
Loom, and plough, and sword, and spade,
With or without your own will bent
To their defence and nourishment.

'Tis to see your children weak
With their mothers pine and peak,
When the winter winds are bleak—
They are dying, whilst I speak.

'Tis to hunger for such diet
As the rich man in his riot
Casts to the fat dogs that lie
Surfeiting beneath his eye.

'Tis to be a slave in soul,
And to hold no strong control
Over your own wills, but be
All that others make of ye.

And at length, when ye complain
With a murmur weak and vain,
'Tis to see the tyrant's crew
Ride over your wives and you:
Blood is on the grass like dew.

PERCY BYSSHE SHELLEY

A Winter Night

It was a chilly winter's night;
   And frost was glittering on the ground,
And evening stars were twinkling bright;
   And from the gloomy plain around
      Came no sound,
But where, within the wood-girt tow'r,
The churchbell slowly struck the hour;

As if that all of human birth
   Had risen to the final day,
And soaring from the wornout earth
   Were called in hurry and dismay,
      Far away;
And I alone of all mankind
Were left in loneliness behind.

WILLIAM BARNES

The Eve of Waterloo

(From Childe Harold)

THERE was a sound of revelry by night,
And Belgium's Capital had gather'd then
Her Beauty and her Chivalry, and bright
The lamps shone o'er fair women and brave men;
A thousand hearts beat happily; and when
Music arose with its voluptuous swell,
Soft eyes look'd love to eyes which spake again,
And all went merry as a marriage bell;
But hush! hark! a deep sound strikes like a rising
    knell!

Did ye not hear it?—No; 'twas but the wind,
Or the car rattling o'er the stormy street;
On with the dance! Let joy be unconfin'd;
No sleep till morn, when Youth and Pleasure meet
To chase the glowing Hours with flying feet.
But hark!—that heavy sound breaks in once more,
As if the clouds its echo would repeat;
And nearer, clearer, deadlier than before!
Arm! Arm! it is—it is—the cannon's opening roar!

LORD BYRON

The Old Sweet Dove of Wiveton

’TWAS the voice of the sweet dove
I heard him move,
I heard him cry:
Love, love.

High in the chestnut tree
Is the nest of the old dove
And there he sits solitary
Crying, Love, love.

The gray of this heavy day
Makes the green of the tree's leaves and the grass
   brighter,
And the flowers of the chestnut tree whiter,
And whiter the flowers of the high cow-parsley.

So still is the air,
So heavy the sky,
You can hear the splash
Of the water falling from the green grass
As Red and Honey push by,
The old dogs,
Gone away, gone hunting by the marsh bogs.

Happy the retriever dogs in their pursuit,
Happy in bog-mud the busy foot.

STEVIE SMITH

Now all is silent, it is silent again,
In the sombre day and the beginning soft rain,
It is a silence made more actual
By the moan from the high tree that is occasional.

Where in his nest above
Still sits the old dove,
Murmuring solitary,
Crying for pain,
Crying most melancholy
Again and again.

STEVIE SMITH

Trees

(From The Faerie Queene.
Book I. Canto i. v. 9)

THE laurel, meed of mighty conquerors
And poets sage; the fir that weepeth still;
The willow, worn of forlorn paramours;
The yew, obedient to the bender's will;
The birch for shafts; the sallow for the mill;
The myrrh sweete-bleeding in the bitter wound;
The warlike beech; the ash for nothing ill;
The fruitful olive; and the platane round;
The carver holm; the maple seldom inward sound.

EDMUND SPENSER

'Who Travels by the Weary Wandering Way'

(*From The Faerie Queene.*
Book I. Canto IX, vv. 39 and 40.)

'WHO travels by the weary wandering way,
To come unto his wished home in haste,
And meets a flood, that doth his passage stay;
Is not great grace to help him over past,
Or free his feet that in the mire stick fast?
Most envious man, that grieves at neighbour's good;
And fond, that joyest in the woe thou hast;
Why wilt not let him pass, that long hath stood
Upon the bank, yet wilt thyself not pass the flood?

'He there does now enjoy eternal rest
And happy ease, which thou dost want and crave,
And farther from it daily wanderest:
What if some little pain the passage have,
That makes frail flesh to fear the bitter wave;
Is not short pain well borne, that brings long ease,
And lays the soul to sleep in quiet grave?
Sleep after toil, port after stormy seas,
Ease after war, death after life, does greatly please.'

EDMUND SPENSER

Thoughts by the Shore

(From The Borough)

Where the small eels that left the deeper way
For the warm shore, within the shallows play;
Where gaping mussels, left upon the mud,
Slope their slow passage to the fallen flood.
Here, dull and hopeless, he'd lie down and trace
How sidelong crabs had scrawl'd their crooked race,
Or sadly listen to the tuneless cry
Of fishing gull or clanging golden-eye;
What time the sea-birds to the marsh would come,
And the loud bittern, from the bull-rush home,
Gave from the salt ditch side the bellowing boom:
He nursed the feelings these dull scenes produce,
And loved to stop beside the opening sluice,
Where the small stream, confined in narrow bound,
Ran with a dull, unvaried, sadd'ning sound.

GEORGE CRABBE

From—Oedipus Coloneus

Chorus: Not to be born at all
Is best, far best that can befall,
Next best, when born, with least delay
To trace the backward way.

SOPHOCLES

The Sick Rose

O ROSE, thou art sick!
The invisible worm,
That flies in the night,
In the howling storm,

Has found out thy bed
Of crimson joy;
And his dark secret love
Does thy life destroy.

WILLIAM BLAKE

From– The Other Man

WHEN the Earth was sick and the Skies were grey,
And the woods were rotted with rain,
The Dead Man rode through the autumn day
To visit his love again.

His love she neither saw nor heard,
So heavy was her shame;
And tho' the babe within her stirred
She knew not that he came.

RUDYARD KIPLING

The Kraken

Below the thunders of the upper deep;
Far, far beneath in the abysmal sea,
His ancient, dreamless, uninvaded sleep
The Kraken sleepeth: faintest sunlights flee
About his shadowy sides: above him swell
Huge sponges of millennial growth and height;
And far away into the sickly light,
From many a wondrous grot and secret cell
Unnumbered and enormous polypi
Winnow with giant arms the slumbering green.
There hath he lain for ages and will lie
Battening upon huge seaworms in his sleep,
Until the latter fire shall heat the deep;
Then once by man and angels to be seen,
In roaring he shall rise and on the surface die.

ALFRED, LORD TENNYSON

The Burning Babe

As I in hoary winter's night
   Stood shivering in the snow,
Surprised I was with sudden heat,
   Which made my heart to glow;
And lifting up a fearful eye
   To view what fire was near,
A pretty babe all burning bright,
   Did in the air appear:
Who, scorchèd with excessive heat,
   Such floods of tears did shed,
As though his floods should quench his flames,
   Which with his tears were fed:
'Alas!' quoth he, 'but newly born,
   In fiery heats I fry,
Yet none approach to warm their hearts
   Or feel my fire, but I!

My faultless breast the furnace is,
   The fuel wounding thorns;
Love is the fire, and sighs the smoke,
   The ashes shames and scorns;
The fuel Justice layeth on,
   And Mercy blows the coals;
The metal in this furnace wrought
   Are men's defilèd souls:
For which, as now on fire I am,
   To work them to their good,
So will I melt into a bath,
   To wash them in my blood.'
With this he vanished out of sight,
   And swiftly shrunk away,
And straight I called unto my mind
   That it was Christmas Day.

ROBERT SOUTHWELL

27

'I think I could turn and live with animals'

(From Song of Myself)

I THINK I could turn and live with animals, they are
   so placid and self-contain'd.
I stand and look at them long and long.
They do not sweat and whine about their condition,
They do not lie awake in the dark and weep for their sins,
They do not make me sick discussing their duty to God,
Not one is dissatisfied, not one is demented with the
   mania of owning things,
Not one kneels to another, nor to his kind that lived
   thousands of years ago,
Not one is respectable and industrious over the whole
   earth.
So they show their relations to me, and I accept them,
They bring me tokens of myself, they evince them
   plainly in their possession.

WALT WHITMAN

The Three Ravens

THERE were three ravens sat on a tree,
They were as black as they might be.

The one of them said to his make,
'Where shall we our breakfast take?'

'Down in yonder greenè field
There lies a knight slain under his shield;

'His hounds they lie down at his feet,
So well do they their master keep;

'His hawks they flie so eagerly,
There is no fowl dare come him nigh.

'Down there comes a fallow doe
As great with young as she might goe.

'She lift up his bloudy head
And kist his wounds that were so red.

'She gat him up upon her back
And carried him to earthen lake.

'She buried him before the prime,
She was dead herself ere evensong time.

'God send every gentleman
Such hounds, such hawks, and such a leman.'

ANONYMOUS

From– The Book of Proverbs

WITHDRAW thy foot from thy neighbour's house;
lest he be weary of thee, and so hate thee.
If thine enemy be hungry, give him bread to eat; and
if he be thirsty, give him water to drink:
For thou shalt heap coals of fire upon his head, and the

Lord shall reward thee.
Where there is no vision, the people perish.

There be three things which are too wonderful for me,
yea, four which I know not:
The way of an eagle in the air; the way of a serpent upon
a rock; the way of a ship in the midst of the sea; and
the way of a man with a maid.

From– The Merchant of Venice

How sweet the moonlight sleeps upon this bank!
Here will we sit, and let the sounds of music
Creep in our ears; soft stillness and the night
Become the touches of sweet harmony.
Sit, Jessica; look, how the floor of heaven
Is thick inlaid with patines of bright gold;
There's not the smallest orb which thou behold'st
But in his motion like an angel sings,
Still quiring to the young-eyed cherubins;
Such harmony is in immortal souls;
But, whilst this muddy vesture of decay
Doth grossly close it in, we cannot hear it.

WILLIAM SHAKESPEARE

From— The Knight's Tale

I AM, thow woost, yet of thy compaignye,
A mayde, and love huntynge and venerye,
And for to walken in the wodës wilde,
And noght to ben a wyf and be with chylde.

GEOFFREY CHAUCER

From— Truth, Balade de Bon Conseyl

G RISILDE is deed, and eek hire pacience,
And both atones buryed in Ytaille;
For which I crie in open audience,
No wedded man so hardy be tassaille
His wyves pacience in hope to fynde
Grisildis, for in certein he shal faille!

GEOFFREY CHAUCER

From— The Clerk of Oxenford's Tale

T HAT thee is sent, receyve in buxumnesse,
The wrastling for this worlde axeth a fall.
Her nis non hom, her nis but wildernesse.
Forth, pilgrim, forth! Forth, beste, out of thy stal,
Know thy contree, look up, thank God of al;
Hold the hye wey, and lat thy ghost thee lede,
And trouthe shall delivere, it is no drede.

GEOFFREY CHAUCER

'The Sun has long been Set'

T HE sun has long been set,
   The stars are out by twos and threes,
The little birds are piping yet
   Among the bushes and the trees;
There's a cuckoo, and one or two thrushes,
And a far-off wind that rushes,
And a sound of water that gushes,
And the cuckoo's sovereign cry
Fills all the hollow of the sky.
   Who would 'go parading'
In London, 'and masquerading',
On such a night of June
With that beautiful soft half-moon,
And all these innocent blisses?
On such a night as this is!

WILLIAM WORDSWORTH

Break, Break, Break

BREAK, break, break,
   On thy cold gray stones, O Sea!
And I would that my tongue could utter
   The thoughts that arise in me.

O well for the fisherman's boy,
   That he shouts with his sister at play!
O well for the sailor lad,
   That he sings in his boat on the bay!

And the stately ships go on
   To their haven under the hill;
But O for the touch of a vanish'd hand,
   And the sound of a voice that is still!

Break, break, break,
   At the foot of thy crags, O Sea!
But the tender grace of a day that is dead
   Will never come back to me.

ALFRED, LORD TENNYSON

From– A Dream of Fair Women

AT length I saw a lady within call,
Stiller than chisell'd marble, standing there;
A daughter of the gods, divinely tall,
And most divinely fair.

Her loveliness with shame and with surprise
Froze my swift speech: she turning on my face
The star-like sorrows of immortal eyes,
Spoke slowly in her place.

'I had great beauty: ask thou not my name:
No one can be more wise than destiny.
Many drew swords and died. Where'er I came
I brought calamity.'

'No marvel, sovereign lady: in fair field
Myself for such a face had boldly died,'
I answer'd free; and turning I appeal'd
To one that stood beside.

But she, with sick and scornful looks averse,
To her full height her stately stature draws;
'My youth,' she said, 'was blasted with a curse:
This woman was the cause.

'I was cut off from hope in that sad place,
Which men call'd Aulis in those iron years:
My father held his hand upon his face;
I, blinded with my tears,

'Still strove to speak: my voice was thick with sighs
As in a dream. Dimly I could descry
The stern black-bearded kings with wolfish eyes,
Waiting to see me die.

'The high masts flicker'd as they lay afloat;
The crowds, the temples, waver'd, and the shore;
The bright death quiver'd at the victim's throat;
Touch'd; and I knew no more.'

ALFRED, LORD TENNYSON

From– Psalm CXXI

I WILL lift up mine eyes unto the hills: from whence cometh my help.

My help cometh even from the Lord: who hath made heaven and earth.

He will not suffer thy foot to be moved: and he that keepeth thee will not sleep.

Behold, he that keepeth Israel: shall neither slumber nor sleep.

The Lord himself is thy keeper: the Lord is thy defence upon thy right hand;

So that the sun shall not burn thee by day: neither the moon by night.

The Lord shall preserve thee from all evil: yea, it is even he that shall keep thy soul.

The Lord shall preserve thy going out, and thy coming in: from this time forth for evermore.

The Frog Prince

I AM a frog
I live under a spell
I live at the bottom
Of a green well.

And here I must wait
Until a maiden places me
On her royal pillow
And kisses me
In her father's palace.

The story is familiar
Everybody knows it well
But do other enchanted people feel as nervous
As I do? The stories do not tell.

Ask if they will be happier
When the changes come
As already they are fairly happy
In a frog's doom?

I have been a frog now
For a hundred years
And in all this time
I have not shed many tears,

I am happy, I like the life,
Can swim for many a mile
(When I have hopped to the river)
And am for ever agile.

And the quietness,
Yes, I like to be quiet
I am habituated
To a quiet life.

But always when I think these thoughts
As I sit in my well
Another thought comes to me and says:
It is part of the 'spell

To be happy
To work up contentment
To make much of being a frog
To fear disenchantment

Says, It will be *heavenly*
To be set free,
Cries, *Heavenly* the girl who disenchants
And the royal times, *heavenly*,
And I think it will be.

Come, then, royal girl and royal times,
Come quickly,
I can be happy until you come
But I cannot be heavenly,
Only disenchanted people
Can be heavenly.

STEVIE SMITH

From– France: An Ode

Y E Clouds! that far above me float and pause,
Whose pathless march no mortal may controul!
Ye Ocean-Waves! that, wheresoe'er ye roll,
Yield homage only to eternal laws!
Ye Woods! that listen to the night-birds singing,
Midway the smooth and perilous slope reclined,
Save when your own imperious branches swinging,
Have made a solemn music of the wind!
Where, like a man beloved of God,
Through glooms, which never woodman trod,
How oft, pursuing fancies holy,
My moonlight way o'er flowering weeds I wound,
Inspired, beyond the guess of folly,
By each rude shape and wild unconquerable sound!
O ye loud Waves! and O ye Forests high!
And O ye Clouds that far above me soared!
Thou rising Sun! thou blue rejoicing Sky!
Yea, every thing that is and will be free!
Bear witness for me, wheresoe'er ye be,
With what deep worship I have still adored
The spirit of divinest Liberty.

SAMUEL TAYLOR COLERIDGE

Annabel Lee

It was many and many a year ago,
    In a kingdom by the sea,
That a maiden there lived whom you may know
    By the name of Annabel Lee;
And this maiden she lived with no other thought
    Than to love and be loved by me.

I was a child and she was a child;
    In this kingdom by the sea;
But we loved with a love that was more than love—
    I and my Annabel Lee;
With a love that the wingèd seraphs of heaven
    Coveted her and me.

And this was the reason that, long ago
    In this kingdom by the sea,
A wind blew out of a cloud, chilling
    My beautiful Annabel Lee;
So that her highborn kinsman came
    And bore her away from me,
To shut her up in a sepulchre
    In this kingdom by the sea.

The angels, not half so happy in heaven,
   Went envying her and me;
Yes! that was the reason (as all men know,
   In this kingdom by the sea)
That the wind came out of the cloud by night,
   Chilling and killing my Annabel Lee.

But our love it was stronger by far than the love
   Of those who were older than we—
   Of many far wiser than we;
And neither the angels in heaven above,
   Nor the demons down under the sea,
Can ever dissever my soul from the soul
   Of the beautiful Annabel Lee.

For the moon never beams without bringing me dreams
   Of the beautiful Annabel Lee;
And the stars never rise, but I feel the bright eyes
   Of the beautiful Annabel Lee;
And so, all the night-tide, I lie down by the side
Of my darling—my darling—my life and my bride,
   In the sepulchre there by the sea,
In her tomb by the sounding sea.

EDGAR ALLAN POE

Hymn to the Seal

(To the tune : 'Soldiers of Christ, arise')

CREATURE of God, thy coat
That lies all black and fine
I do admire, as on a sunny
Rock to see thee climb.

When thou wast young thy coat
Was pale with spots upon it
But now in single black it lies
And thou, Seal, liest on it.

What bliss abounds to view
God's creatures in their prime
Climb in full coat upon a rock
To breathe and to recline.

STEVIE SMITH

The Deserted House

THERE'S no smoke in the chimney,
And the rain beats on the floor;
There's no glass in the window,
There's no wood in the door;
The heather grows behind the house,
And the sand lies before.

No hand hath trained the ivy,
The walls are gray and bare;
The boats upon the sea sail by,
Nor ever tarry here.
No beast of the field comes nigh,
Nor any bird of the air.

MARY COLERIDGE

From– Isabella

Wɪᴛʜ her two brothers this fair lady dwelt,
Enriched from ancestral merchandise,
And for them many a weary hand did swelt
In torched mines and noisy factories,
And many once proud-quivered loins did melt
In blood from stinging whip;—with hollow eyes
Many all day in dazzling river stood,
To take the rich-ored driftings of the flood.

For them the Ceylon diver held his breath,
And went all naked to the hungry shark;
For them his ears gush'd blood; for them in death
The seal on the cold ice with piteous bark
Lay full of darts; for them alone did seethe
A thousand men in troubles wide and dark:
Half-ignorant, they turned an easy wheel,
That set sharp racks at work, to pinch and peel.

Why were they proud? Because their marble founts
Gush'd with more pride than do a wretch's tears?—
Why were they proud? Because fair orange-mounts
Were of more soft ascent than lazar stairs?—
Why were they proud? Because red-lin'd accounts
Were richer than the songs of Grecian years?—
Why were they proud? again we ask aloud,
Why in the name of Glory were they proud?

JOHN KEATS

The Foggy Foggy Dew

Oh I am a bachelor, I live all alone,
And I work at the weaver's trade,
And the only, only thing that I ever did wrong
Was to woo a fair young maid;
I wooed her in the winter time,
And in the summer too;
And the only, only thing that I ever did wrong
Was to keep her from the foggy, foggy dew.

One night she came to my bedside
Where I lay fast asleep,
She laid her head upon my bed,
And she began to weep;
She sobbed, she sighed, she damn near died,
She said, 'What shall I do?'
So I hauled her into bed and I covered up her head,
For to keep her from the foggy, foggy dew.

Oh I am a bachelor, I live with my son,
And we work at the weaver's trade,
And every, every time that I look into his eyes,
He reminds me of that fair young maid,
He reminds me in the winter time,
And in the summer too,
Of the many, many times that I held her in my arms
Just to keep her from the foggy, foggy dew.

ANONYMOUS

Adlestrop

Yes, I remember Adlestrop—
The name, because one afternoon
Of heat the express-train drew up there
Unwontedly. It was late June.

The steam hissed. Someone cleared his throat.
No one left and no one came
On the bare platform. What I saw
Was Adlestrop—only the name

And willows, willow-herb, and grass,
And meadowsweet, and haycocks dry,
No whit less still and lonely fair
Than the high cloudlets in the sky.

And for that minute a blackbird sang
Close by, and round him, mistier,
Farther and farther, all the birds
Of Oxfordshire and Gloucestershire.

EDWARD THOMAS

From– Epistle to Davie

THE sacred lowe of weel-placed love,
Luxuriantly indulge it;
But never tempt th' illicit rove,
Tho' naething should divulge it:
I waive the quantum of the sin,
The hazard of concealing;
But, och! it hardens a' within,
And petrifies the feeling.

ROBERT BURNS

Queen Elizabeth Tudor, as a girl, On trial for heresy

HIS was the Word that spake it
He took the Bread and brake it
And what that Word doth make it
I do believe and take it.

From– The Winter's Tale

Autolycus: Jog on, jog on, the footpath way,
And merrily hent the stile-a:
A merry heart goes all the day,
Your sad tires in a mile-a.

WILLIAM SHAKESPEARE

From– The Office of the Holy Cross

The Hymn

THE third hour's deafen'd with the cry
Of 'Crucify Him, crucify.'
So goes the vote (nor ask them, why?)
'Live Barabbas! and let God die.'
But there is wit in wrath, and they will try
A 'Hail' more cruel than their 'Crucify.'
For while in sport He wears a spiteful crown,
The serious showers along His decent Face run
sadly down.

The Antiphon

Christ when He died
Deceived the Cross;
And on Death's side
Threw all the loss.
The captive World awaked and found
The prisoner loose, the jailer bound.

The Versicle

Lo, we adore Thee,
Dread Lamb! and fall
Thus low before Thee.

The Responsory

'Cause by the covenant of Thy cross
Thou hast saved at once the whole World's loss.

RICHARD CRASHAW

Sonnet XCIV

They that have power to hurt and will do none,
That do not do the thing they most do show,
Who, moving others, are themselves as stone,
Unmoved, cold, and to temptation slow;
They rightly do inherit heaven's graces,
And husband nature's riches from expense;
They are the lords and owners of their faces,
Others but stewards of their excellence.
The summer's flower is to the summer sweet,
Though to itself it only live and die,
But if that flower with base infection meet,
The basest weed outbraves his dignity:
For sweetest things turn sourest by their deeds;
Lilies that fester smell far worse than weeds.

WILLIAM SHAKESPEARE

A Peck of Gold

Dust always blowing about the town,
Except when sea-fog laid it down,
And I was one of the children told
Some of the blowing dust was gold.

All the dust the wind blew high
Appeared like gold in the sunset sky,
But I was one of the children told
Some of the dust was really gold.

Such was life in the Golden Gate:
Gold dusted all we drank and ate,
And I was one of the children told,
'We all must eat our peck of gold.'

ROBERT FROST

The Revelation

An idle poet, here and there,
Looks round him, but, for all the rest,
The world, unfathomably fair,
Is duller than a witling's jest.

Love wakes men, once a lifetime each;
They lift their heavy lids and look;
And, lo, what one sweet page can teach
They read with joy, then shut the book.

And some give thanks, and some blaspheme,
And most forget; but either way,
That, and the child's unheeded dream,
Is all the light of all their day.

COVENTRY PATMORE

Engraved on the Collar of a Dog, which I gave to His Royal Highness

I am his Highness' dog at Kew;
Pray tell me, sir, whose dog are you?

ALEXANDER POPE

Composed upon Westminster Bridge, September 3rd 1802

EARTH hath not anything to show more fair:
Dull would he be of soul who could pass by
A sight so touching in its majesty:
This city now doth like a garment wear
The beauty of the morning; silent, bare,
Ships, towers, domes, theatres, and temples lie
Open unto the fields, and to the sky;
All bright and glittering in the smokeless air.
Never did sun more beautifully steep
In his first splendour valley, rock, or hill;
Ne'er saw I, never felt, a calm so deep!
The river glideth at his own sweet will:
Dear God! the very houses seem asleep;
And all that mighty heart is lying still!

WILLIAM WORDSWORTH

A Green Cornfield

THE earth was green, the sky was blue:
I saw and heard one sunny morn
A skylark hang between the two,
    A singing speck above the corn;

A stage below, in gay accord,
    White butterflies danced on the wing,
And still the singing skylark soared,
    And silent sank and soared to sing.

The cornfield stretched a tender green
    To right and left beside my walks;
I knew he had a nest unseen
    Somewhere among the million stalks.

And as I paused to hear his song
    While swift the sunny movements slid,
Perhaps his mate sat listening long,
    And listening longer than I did.

CHRISTINA ROSSETTI

Epitaph on a Hare

HERE lies, whom hound did ne'er pursue,
Nor swifter greyhound follow,
Whose foot ne'er tainted morning dew,
Nor ear heard huntsman's halloo;

Old Tiney, surliest of his kind,
Who, nursed with tender care,
And to domestic bounds confined,
Was still a wild Jack hare.

Though duly from my hand he took
His pittance every night,
He did it with a jealous look,
And, when he could, would bite.

His diet was of wheaten bread,
And milk, and oats, and straw;
Thistles, or lettuces instead,
With sand to scour his maw.

On twigs of hawthorn he regaled,
On pippins' russet peel,
And, when his juicy salads fail'd,
Sliced carrot pleased him well.

A Turkey carpet was his lawn,
Whereon he loved to bound,
To skip and gambol like a fawn,
And swing his rump around.

His frisking was at evening hours,
For then he lost his fear,
But most before approaching showers,
Or when a storm drew near.

Eight years and five round rolling moons
He thus saw steal away,
Dozing out all his idle noons,
And everynight at play.

I kept him for his humour's sake,
For he would oft beguile
My heart of thoughts that made it ache,
And force me to a smile.

But now beneath his walnut shade
He finds his long last home,
And waits, in snug concealment laid,
Till gentler Puss shall come.

He, still more agèd, feels the shocks
From which no care can save,
And, partner once of Tiney's box,
Must soon partake his grave.

WILLIAM COWPER

To-Whit To-Who

WHEN Isicles hang by the wall,
   And Dicke the shepheard blowes his naile,
And Tom beares Logges into the hall,
   And Milke comes frozen home in paile:
When blood is nipt, and waies be fowle,
Then nightly sings the staring Owle,
      To-whit to-who
      A merrie note,
While greasie Jone doth keele the pot.

When all aloud the winde doth blow,
   And coffing drownes the Parson's saw;
And birds sit brooding in the snow,
   And Marrian's nose lookes red and raw;
When roasted Crabs hisse in the bowle,
Then nightly sings the staring Owle,
      To-whit to-who
      A merrie note,
While greasie Jone doth keele the pot.

WILLIAM SHAKESPEARE

From— The Book of Job

Where wast thou when I laid the foundations of
the earth? declare, if thou hast understanding.
When the morning stars sang together, and all the sons
of God shouted for joy?
Hast thou entered into the springs of the sea? or hast
thou walked in the search of the depth?
Hast thou entered into the treasures of the snow? or
hast thou seen the treasures of the hail?
Canst thou bind the sweet influence of the Pleiades, or
loose the bands of Orion?
Who can number the clouds in wisdom? or who can
stay the bottles of heaven?
Wilt thou hunt the prey for the lion? or fill the appetite
of the young lions,
When they couch in their dens, and abide in the covert
to lie in wait?
Who provideth for the raven his food? when his young
ones cry unto God, they wander for lack of meat.

From— The Poet's Mind

Vex not thou the poet's mind
With thy shallow wit:
Vex not thou the poet's mind;
For thou canst not fathom it.

ALFRED, LORD TENNYSON

Acquainted with the Night

I HAVE been one acquainted with the night.
I have walked out in rain—and back in rain.
I have outwalked the furthest city light.

I have looked down the saddest city lane.
I have passed by the watchman on his beat
And dropped my eyes, unwilling to explain.

I have stood still and stopped the sound of feet
When far away an interrupted cry
Came over houses from another street,

But not to call me back or say goodbye;
And further still at an unearthly height,
One luminary clock against the sky

Proclaimed the time was neither wrong nor right.
I have been one acquainted with the night.

ROBERT FROST

I Remember

I REMEMBER, I remember,
The house where I was born,
The little window where the sun
Came peeping in at morn;
He never came a wink too soon,
Nor brought too long a day;
But now, I often wish the night
Had borne my breath away!

I remember, I remember,
The roses, red and white,
The vi'lets, and the lily-cups,
Those flowers made of light!
The lilacs where the robin built,
And where my brother set
The laburnum on his birth-day,—
The tree is living yet!

I remember, I remember,
Where I used to swing,
And thought the air must rush as fresh
To swallows on the wing;
My spirit flew in feathers then,
That is so heavy now,
And summer pools could hardly cool
The fever on my brow!

I remember, I remember,
The fir trees dark and high;
I used to think their slender tops
Were close against the sky:
It was a childish ignorance,
But now 'tis little joy
To know I'm farther off from heaven
Than when I was a boy.

THOMAS HOOD

Deadman's Dirge

Prayer unsaid, and Mass unsung,
Deadman's dirge must still be rung:
  Dingle-dong, the dead-bells sound!
  Merman chant his dirge around!

Wash him bloodless, smooth him fair,
Stretch his limbs, and sleek his hair:
  Dingle-dong, the dead-bells go!
  Mermen swing them to and fro!

In the wormless sand shall he
Feast for no foul glutton be:
  Dingle-dong, the dead-bells chime!
  Mermen keep the tone and time!

We must with a tombstone brave
Shut the shark out from his grave:
  Dingle-dong, the dead-bells toll!
  Mermen dirgers ring his knoll!

Such a slab will we lay o'er him,
All the dead shall rise before him:
  Dingle-dong, the dead-bells boom!
  Mermen lay him in his tomb!

GEORGE DARLEY

So to Fatness Come

Poor human race that must
Feed on pain, or choose
Another dish and hunger worse.

There is also a cup of pain, for
You to drink all up, or
Setting it aside for sweeter drink
Thirst evermore.

I am thy friend, I wish
You to sup full of the dish
I give you, and the drink,
And so to fatness come more than you think,
In health of opened heart, and know peace.

Grief spake these words to me in a dream, I thought
He spoke no more than grace allowed,
And no less than truth.

STEVIE SMITH

From— Ode. Intimations of Immortality

Our birth is but a sleep and a forgetting;
The Soul that rises with us, our life's Star,
    Hath had elsewhere its setting,
        And cometh from afar:
    Not in entire forgetfulness,
    And not in utter nakedness,
But trailing clouds of glory, do we come
    From God, who is our home.

WILLIAM WORDSWORTH

71

From– The Winter's Tale

Perdita: . . . . Here's flowers for you;
Hot lavender, mints, savory, marjoram;
The marigold, that goes to bed wi' the sun,
And with him rises weeping: these are flowers
Of middle summer, and I think they are given
To men of middle age. You're very welcome.

Camillo: I should leave grazing, were I of your flock,
And only live by gazing.

Perdita: . . . . Out, alas!
You'd be so lean, that blasts of January
Would blow you through and through. Now,
my fair'st friend,
I would I had some flowers o' the spring that
might
Become your time of day; and yours, and
yours,
That wear upon your virgin branches yet
Your maidenheads growing: O Proserpina!
For the flowers now that frighted thou
let'st fall
From Dis's waggon! daffodils,
That come before the swallow dares, and take
The winds of March with beauty; violets dim,
But sweeter than the lids of Juno's eyes
Or Cytherea's breath; pale prime-roses,
That die unmarried, ere they can behold
Bright Phoebus in his strength, a malady
Most incident to maids; bold oxlips and
The crown imperial; lilies of all kinds,
The flower-de-luce being one.

WILLIAM SHAKESPEARE

John Peel

D'YE ken John Peel with his coat so gray?
D'ye ken John Peel at the break of the day?
D'ye ken John Peel when he's far, far away,
With his hounds and his horn in the morning?

'Twas the sound of his horn called me from my bed,
And the cry of his hounds has me oft-times led,
For Peel's *View-hollo* would waken the dead,
Or a fox from his lair in the morning.

D'ye ken that bitch whose tongue is death?
D'ye ken her sons of peerless faith?
D'ye ken that a fox with his last breath
Cursed them all as he died in the morning?

Yes, I ken John Peel and Ruby too
Ranter and Royal and Bellman as true;
From the drag to the chase, from the chase to a view,
From a view to the death in the morning.

And I've followed John Peel both often and far
O'er the rasper-fence and the gate and the bar,
From Low Denton Holme up to Scratchmere Scar,
When we vied for the brush in the morning.

Then here's to John Peel with my heart and soul,
Come fill—fill to him another strong bowl;
And we'll follow John Peel through fair and through foul,
While we're waked by his horn in the morning.

'Twas the sound of his horn called me from my bed,
And the cry of his hounds has me oft-times led,
For Peel's *View-hollo* would waken the dead
Or a fox from his lair in the morning.

JOHN WOODCOCK GRAVES

The Waning Moon

AND like a dying lady, lean and pale,
Who totters forth, wrapt in a gauzy veil,
Out of her chamber, led by the insane
And feeble wanderings of her fading brain,
The moon arose up in the murky East,
A white and shapeless mass.

PERCY BYSSHE SHELLEY

From– The Book of Proverbs

THERE be four things which are little upon the earth,
but they are exceeding wise:
The ants are a people not strong, yet they prepare their
meat in the summer;
The conies are but a feeble folk, yet make they their
houses in the rocks;
The locusts have no king, yet go they forth all of them
by bands;
The spider taketh hold with her hands, and is in kings'
palaces.

From— Prometheus Unbound

On a poet's lips I slept
Dreaming like a love-adept
In the sound his breathing kept;
Nor seeks nor finds he mortal blisses,
But feeds on the aerial kisses
Of shapes that haunt thought's wildernesses.
He will watch from dawn to gloom
The lake-reflected sun illume
The yellow bees in the ivy-bloom,
Nor heed nor see, what things they be;
But from these create he can
Forms more real than living man
Nurslings of immortality!

PERCY BYSSHE SHELLEY

The maidens came
When I was in my mother's bower;
I had all that I would.
The bailey beareth the bell away;
The lily, the rose, the rose I lay.

The silver is white, red is the gold;
The robes they lay in fold.
The bailey beareth the bell away;
The lily, the rose, the rose I lay.

And through the glass window shines the sun.
How should I love, and I so young?
The bailey beareth the bell away;
The lily, the rose, the rose I lay.

ANONYMOUS

Of God's great power in the leviathan

(From The Book of Job)

CANST thou draw out leviathan with an hook? or his tongue with a cord which thou lettest down?

Canst thou put an hook into his nose? or bore his jaw through with a thorn?

Will he make many supplications unto thee? will he speak soft words unto thee?

Will he make a covenant with thee? wilt thou take him for a servant for ever?

Wilt thou play with him as with a bird? or wilt thou bind him for thy maidens?

I will not conceal his parts, nor his power, nor his comely proportion.

Who can open the doors of his face? his teeth are terrible round about.

His scales are his pride, shut up together as with a close seal.

Out of his mouth go burning lamps, and sparks of fire leap out.

His breath kindleth coals, and a flame goeth out of his mouth.

The sword of him that layeth at him cannot hold: the spear, the dart, nor the habergeon.

Darts are counted as stubble: he laugheth at the shaking of a spear.

Sharp stones are under him: he spreadeth sharp pointed things upon the mire.

He maketh the deep to boil like a pot: he maketh the sea like a pot of ointment.

He maketh a path to shine after him; one would think the deep to be hoary.

Upon earth there is not his like, who is made without fear.

He beholdeth all high things: he is a king over all the children of pride.

'I Had a Dove'

I HAD a dove and the sweet dove died;
   And I have thought it died of grieving:
O what could it grieve for? Its feet were tied,
With a silken thread of my own hand's weaving;
   Sweet little red feet! why should you die—
Why should you leave me, sweet bird! Why?
You lived alone in the forest-tree,
Why, pretty thing! would you not live with me?
I kissed you oft and gave you white peas;
Why not live sweetly, as in the green trees?

JOHN KEATS

From— Rain in Summer

How beautiful is the rain!
After the dust and heat,
In the broad and fiery street,
In the narrow lane,
How beautiful is the rain!

How it clatters along the roofs,
Like the tramp of hoofs!
How it gushes and struggles out
From the throat of the overflowing spout!

Across the window-pane
It pours and pours;
And swift and wide,
With a muddy tide,
Like a river down the gutter roars
The rain, the welcome rain!

H. W. LONGFELLOW

From– The Rime of the Ancient Mariner

THE fair breeze blew, the white foam flew,
The furrow followed free;
We were the first that ever burst
Into that silent sea.

Down dropt the breeze, the sails dropt down,
'Twas sad as sad could be;
And we did speak only to break
The silence of the sea!

All in a hot and copper sky,
The bloody Sun, at noon,
Right up above the mast did stand,
No bigger than the Moon.

Day after day, day after day,
We stuck, nor breath nor motion;
As idle as a painted ship
Upon a painted ocean.

The very deep did rot: O Christ!
That ever this should be!
Yea, slimy things did crawl with legs
Upon the slimy sea.

About, about, in reel and rout
The death-fires danced at night;
The water, like a witch's oils,
Burnt green, and blue and white.

And some in dreams assurèd were
Of the spirit that plagued us so;
Nine fathom deep he had followed us
From the land of mist and snow.

SAMUEL TAYLOR COLERIDGE

From– King John

King John. Act IV, Scene III
(The boy Prince Arthur lies dead on the ground having
thrown himself from the castle wall)

Bastard (to Hubert)
     Go, bear him in thine arms.
I am amaz'd, methinks, and lose my way
Among the thorns and dangers of this world.
How easy dost thou take all England up!
. . . .
. . . . Bear away that child
And follow me with speed: I'll to the king.

WILLIAM SHAKESPEARE

'A Widow Bird'

A widow bird sat mourning for her love
  Upon a wintry bough;
The frozen wind kept on above,
  The freezing stream below.

There was no leaf upon the forest bare,
  No flower upon the ground
And little motion in the air
  Except the mill-wheel's sound.

PERCY BYSSHE SHELLEY

The Ruined Maid

O'MELIA, my dear, this does everything crown!
Who would have supposed I should meet you in Town?
And whence such fair garments, such prosperi-ty?'—
'O didn't you know I'd been ruined?' said she.

'You left us in tatters, without shoes or socks,
Tired of digging potatoes, and spudding up docks:
And now you've gay bracelets and bright feathers three!'
'Yes: that's how we dress when we're ruined,' said she.

'At home in the barton you said "thee" and "thou",
And "thik oon" and "theas oon," and "t'other"; but now
Your talking quite fits 'ee for high compa-ny!'—
'Some polish is gained with one's ruin,' said she.

'Your hands were like paws then, your face blue and
    bleak
But now I'm bewitched by your delicate cheek,
And your little gloves fit as on any la-dy!'—
'We never do work when we're ruined,' said she.

'You used to call home-life a hag-ridden dream,
And you'd sigh, and you'd sock; but at present you seem
To know not of megrims or melanchol-ly!'—
'True. One's pretty lively when ruined,' said she.

—'I wish I had feathers, a fine sweeping gown,
And a delicate face, and could strut about Town!'—
'My dear—a raw country girl, such as you be,
Cannot quite expect that. You ain't ruined,' said she.

THOMAS HARDY

The Occasional Yarrow

It was a mile of greenest grass
Whereon a little stream did pass,
   The Occasional Yarrow

Only in every seventh year
Did this pretty stream appear,
   The Occasional Yarrow

Wading and warbling in its beds
Of grass decked out with daisy heads,
   The Occasional Yarrow

There, in my seventh year and this sweet stream's,
I wandered happily (as happy gleams
   The Occasional Yarrow)

Though now to Memory alone
I can call up thy lovely form,
   Occasional Yarrow

I still do bless thy Seventh days
Bless thy sweet name and all who praise
   The Occasional Yarrow.

STEVIE SMITH

Lord Rendal

OH where have you been to, Lord Rendal my son?
Oh where have you been to, my sweet pretty one?
I've been to my sweetheart, Mother,
I've been to my sweetheart, Mother, make my bed soon
For I'm sick to my heart and I fain would lie down.

What gat ye to eat there, Lord Rendal my son?
What gat ye to eat there, my sweet pretty one?
Eels, Mother, eels, Mother, make my bed soon,
For I'm sick to my heart and I fain would lie down.

What colour were they, Lord Rendal my son?
What colour were they, my sweet pretty one?
All spickled and spackled, Mother.
All spickled and spackled, Mother, make my bed soon
For I'm sick to my heart and I fain would lie down.

Oh that was strong poison, Lord Rendal my son,
Oh that was strong poison, my sweet pretty one;
Yes, I am poisoned, Mother,
Yes, I am poisoned, Mother, make my bed soon
For I'm sick to my heart and I fain would lie down.

What will you leave your brother, Lord Rendal my son?
What will you leave your brother, my sweet pretty one?
My clothes and my jewels, Mother,
My clothes and my jewels, Mother, make my bed soon
For I'm sick to my heart and I fain would lie down.

What will you leave your sweetheart, Lord Rendal my
    son?
What will you leave your sweetheart, my sweet pretty
    one?
A rope to hang her, Mother,
A rope to hang her, Mother, make my bed soon
For I'm sick to my heart and I fain would lie down.

ANONYMOUS

From– Lays of Ancient Rome

From the Battle of Lake Regillus

FROM every warlike city
That boasts the Latian name,
Foredoomed to dogs and vultures,
That gallant army came;
From Setia's purple vineyards,
From Norba's ancient wall,
From the white streets of Tusculum,
The proudest town of all;
From where the witch's fortress
O'erhangs the dark-blue seas,
From the still glassy lake that sleeps
Beneath Aricia's trees—
Those trees in whose dim shadows
The ghastly priest doth reign,
The priest who slew the slayer,
And shall himself be slain.

Herminius's Horse

But, like a graven image,
Black Auster kept his place,
And ever wistfully he looked
Into his master's face.
The raven-mane that daily,
With pats and fond caresses,
The young Herminia washed and combed,
And twisted in even tresses,
And decked with coloured ribands,
From her own gay attire,
Hung sadly o'er her father's corpse
In carnage and in mire.

LORD MACAULAY

85

From– The Book of Ecclesiastes

LIVE joyfully with the wife whom thou lovest all the days of the life of thy vanity, which he hath given thee under the sun, all the days of thy vanity: for that is thy portion in this life, and in thy labour which thou takest under the sun.
Whatsoever thy hand findeth to do, do it with thy might; for there is no work, nor device, nor knowledge, nor wisdom, in the grave, whither thou goest.

I returned, and saw under the sun, that the race is not to the swift, nor the battle to the strong, neither yet bread to the wise, nor yet riches to men of understanding, nor yet favour to men of skill; but time and chance happeneth to them all.

The Maldive Shark

ABOUT the Shark, phlegmatical one,
Pale sot of the Maldive sea,
The sleek little pilot fish, azure and slim,
How alert in attendance he.
From his saw-pit of mouth, from his charnel of maw,
They have nothing of harm to dread,
But liquidly glide on his ghastly flank
Or before his Gorgonian head;
Or lurk in the port of serrated teeth
In white triple tiers of glittering gates,

And there find a haven when peril's abroad,
An asylum in jaws of the Fates!
They are friends; and friendly they guide him to prey
Yet never partake of the treat—
Eyes and brains to the dotard lethargic and dull,
Pale ravener of horrible meat.

HERMAN MELVILLE

'Now Came Still Evening On'

(From Paradise Lost)

Now came still Evening on, and Twilight gray
Had in her sober livery all things clad;
Silence accompanied, for beast and bird,
They to their grassy couch, these to their nests
Were slunk, all but the wakeful nightingale;
She all night long her amorous descant sung;
Silence was pleas'd: now glow'd the firmament
With living sapphires: Hesperus that led
The starry host, rode brightest, till the Moon
Rising in clouded majesty, at length
Apparent Queen unveil'd her peerless light,
And o'er the dark her silver mantle threw.

JOHN MILTON

Midnight on the Great Western

Iɴ the third-class seat sat the journeying boy,
 And the roof-lamp's oily flame
Played down on his listless form and face,
Bewrapt past knowing to what he was going,
 Or whence he came.

In the band of his hat the journeying boy
 Had a ticket stuck; and a string
Around his neck bore the key of his box,
That twinkled gleams of the lamp's sad beams
 Like a living thing.

What past can be yours, O journeying boy
 Towards a world unknown,
Who calmly, as if incurious quite
On all at stake, can undertake
 This plunge alone?

Knows your soul a sphere, O journeying boy,
 Our rude realms far above,
Whence with spacious vision you mark and mete
This region of sin that you find you in,
 But are not of?

THOMAS HARDY

88

*From—*Adieu! Farewell Earth's Bliss!

Adieu! farewell earth's bliss!
This world uncertain is:
Fond are life's lustful joys,
Death proves them all but toys.
None from his darts can fly:
I am sick, I must die—
    LORD, HAVE MERCY ON US!

Rich men, trust not in wealth,
Gold cannot buy your health;
Physic himself must fade:
All things to end are made;
The plague full swift goes by:
I am sick: I must die—
    LORD, HAVE MERCY ON US!

Beauty is but a flower
Which wrinkles will devour:
Brightness falls from the air;
Queens have died young and fair;
Dust hath closed Helen's eye:
I am sick, I must die—
    LORD, HAVE MERCY ON US!

THOMAS NASHE

From– The Masque of Anarchy

I MET Murder on the way—
He had a mask like Castlereagh—
Very smooth he looked, yet grim;
Seven bloodhounds followed him:

All were fat; and well they might
Be in admirable plight,
For one by one, and two by two,
He tossed them human hearts to chew,
Which from his wide cloak he drew.

Next came Fraud, and he had on,
Like Lord E——, an ermined gown;
His big tears, for he wept well,
Turned to mill-stones as they fell;

And the little children, who
Round his feet played to and fro,
Thinking every tear a gem,
Had their brains knocked out by them.
. . .
Last came Anarchy; he rode
On a white horse, splashed with blood;
He was pale even to the lips,
Like Death in the Apocalypse.
. . .
Then all cried with one accord,
'Thou art King, and God, and Lord;
Anarchy, to thee we bow,
Be thy name made holy now!'

And Anarchy, the skeleton,
Bowed and grinned to every one,
As well as if his education
Had cost ten millions to the nation.

   . . .

When one fled past, a maniac maid,
And her name was Hope, she said:
But she looked more like Despair;
And she cried out in the air:

'My father, Time, is weak and grey
With waiting for a better day.'

PERCY BYSSHE SHELLEY

Remember Thee!
Remember Thee!

Lines to Caroline Lamb

REMEMBER thee! remember thee!
Till Lethe quench life's burning stream,
Remorse and shame shall cling to thee,
And haunt thee like a feverish dream!

Remember thee! Ay, doubt it not,
Thy husband too shall think of thee:
By neither shalt thou be forgot,
Thou *false* to him, thou *fiend* to me!

LORD BYRON

From— Auguries of Innocence

EVERY night and every morn
Some to misery are born.
Every morn and every night
Some are born to sweet delight
Some are born to sweet delight
Some are born to endless night.

God appears, and God is Light,
To those poor souls who dwell in Night;
But does a Human Form display
To those who dwell in realms of Day.

WILLIAM BLAKE

Gnomic Verses

Eternity

HE who bends to himself a Joy
Doth the winged life destroy;
But he who kisses the Joy as it flies
Lives in Eternity's sunrise.

Riches

THE countless gold of a merry heart,
The rubies and pearls of a loving eye,
The indolent never can bring to the mart,
Nor the secret hoard up in his treasury.

The Angel that presided o'er my birth
Said 'Little creature, form'd of joy and mirth,
Go, love without the help of anything on earth.'

WILLIAM BLAKE

Feare No More

FEARE no more the heate o' th' Sun,
Nor the fureous Winters rages,
Thou thy worldly task hast don,
Home art gon, and tane thy wages.
Golden Lads and Girles all must,
As Chimney-Sweepers, come to dust.

Feare no more the frown o' th' Great,
Thou art past the Tirants stroake,
Care no more to cloath, and eate,
To thee the Reede is as the Oake:
The Scepter, Learning, Physicke must,
All follow this, and come to dust.

Feare no more the Lightning flash,
Nor the all-dreaded Thunder-stone,
Feare not Slander, Censure rash,
Thou hast finished joy and mone.
All Lovers young, all Lovers must,
Consigne to thee, and come to dust . . .

WILLIAM SHAKESPEARE

Hiawatha's Fishing

At the stern sat Hiawatha,
With his fishing-line of cedar;
In his plumes the breeze of morning
Played as in the hemlock branches;
On the bows, with tail erected,
Sat the squirrel, Adjidaumo;
In his fur the breeze of morning
Played as in the prairie grasses.
On the white sand of the bottom
Lay the monster Mishe-Nahma,
Lay the sturgeon, King of Fishes;
Through his gills he breathed the water,
With his fins he fanned and winnowed,
With his tail he swept the sand-floor.
There he lay in all his armour;
On each side a shield to guard him,
Plates of bone upon his forehead,
Down his sides and back and shoulders
Plates of bone with spines projecting!
Painted was he with his war-paints,
Stripes of yellow, red and azure,
Spots of brown and spots of sable;
And he lay there on the bottom,
Fanning with his fins of purple,
As above him Hiawatha
In his birch-canoe came sailing,
With his fishing-line of cedar.

H. W LONGFELLOW

Two Songs of a Fool

I

A SPECKLED cat and a tame hare
Eat at my hearthstone
And sleep there;
And both look up to me alone
For learning and defence
As I look up to Providence.

I start out of my sleep to think
Some day I may forget
Their food and drink;
Or, the house door left unshut,
The hare may run till it's found
The horn's sweet note and the tooth of the hound.

I bear a burden that might well try
Men that do all by rule,
And what can I
That am a wandering-witted fool
But pray to God that He ease
My great responsibilities?

II

I slept on my three-legged stool by the fire,
The speckled cat slept on my knee;
We never thought to enquire
Where the brown hare might be,
And whether the door were shut.
Who knows how she drank the wind
Stretched up on two legs from the mat,
Before she had settled her mind
To drum with her heel and to leap?
Had I but awakened from sleep
And called her name, she had heard,
It may be, and had not stirred,
That now, it may be, has found
The horn's sweet note and the tooth of the hound.

W. B. YEATS

We'll go no more A-roving

So, we'll go no more a-roving
   So late into the night,
Though the heart be still as loving,
   And the moon be still as bright.

For the sword outwears its sheath,
   And the soul wears out the breast,
And the heart must pause to breathe,
   And love itself have rest.

Though the night was made for loving,
   And the day returns too soon,
Yet we'll go no more a-roving
   By the light of the moon.

LORD BYRON

Here a Little Child I Stand

Here a little child I stand,
Heaving up my either hand;
Cold as Paddocks though they be,
Here I lift them up to Thee,
For a Benizon to fall
On our meat, and on us all.
            Amen.

ROBERT HERRICK